STECK-VAUGHN
Elements of Reading

Level B

Vocabulary

Isabel L. Beck, Ph.D., and Margaret G. McKeown, Ph.D.

This book belongs to

_____

HarcourtAchieve
Rigby • Steck-Vaughn

www.HarcourtAchieve.com
1.800.531.5015

Acknowledgments

Editorial Director Stephanie Muller

Lead Editor Terra Tarango

Editor Jen Rassler

Design Team Cynthia Ellis, Alexandra Corona, Joan Cunningham

Production Team Mychael Ferris-Pacheco, Paula Schumann, Alan Klemp

Editorial, Design, and Production Development The Quarasan Group, Inc.

Illustrations: Susan Banta 83, 92; Amy Bishop 18; Lindy Burnett 16, 58; Priscilla Burris 72; Rebecca Bush 12, 70; Roberta Collier-Morales 4; Laurie Conley 56; Nancy Didion iii, 88, 91; Angela Donato 35; Drew-Brook-Cormack Assoc. 51, 86; Teddy Edinjiklian 52; Doreen Gay-Kassel 20, 47; Jerry Harston 54, 90; Meryl Henderson 14; Richard Hoit 98; Nicole in den Bosch 99; Diana Kizlauskas 24, 78; Barbara Lanza 22; Jeff LeVan 30, 68; Brian Lies 43, 76, 95; Diana McFarland 6, 42, 62; Carol Newsom 40, 96; Ed Olson 8, 87; Kevin O'Malley 64, 74; Philomena O'Neill 26; David Opie 79; Mark Page 48; Lori Pandy 71; Karen Pellaton 80; Gary Phillips 32, 66; Yuri Salzman 28; Janice Skivington-Wood 39, 82; Bridget Starr Taylor iv, 31; Neecy Twinem 60, 94; Laura Watson 1, 38

ISBN 0-7398-8447-6

Printed in China   2   3   4   5   6   7   8   9   10   985   08   07   06   05   04

Dear Teacher,

This Student Book is full of lively, fun-filled activities that provide ample opportunities for children to practice using new words.

The vocabulary words in this book are meant to increase children's oral vocabulary skills, so the activities are designed to be led by the teacher. Use the teacher notes at the bottom of each page in conjunction with the Word Chats in the Teacher's Guide to facilitate engaging discussions surrounding these activities.

While this book is for children, we hope that you will have fun, too! The more you use and have fun with new words, the more children will enjoy and use them, too.

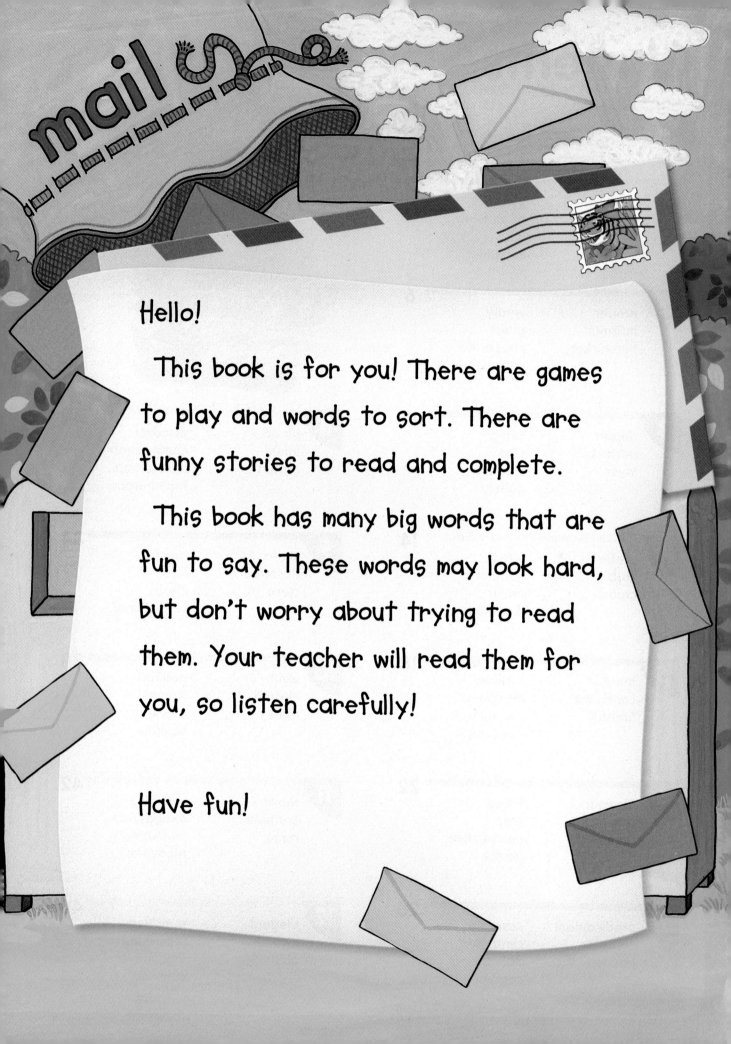

Hello!

This book is for you! There are games to play and words to sort. There are funny stories to read and complete.

This book has many big words that are fun to say. These words may look hard, but don't worry about trying to read them. Your teacher will read them for you, so listen carefully!

Have fun!

Contents

1 Write the words that have to do with **shelter**.

watch

house

belt

room

_____

_____

2 Write the words that have to do with **fleet**.

_____

_____

fast

slow

ready

quick

3 Write the words that have to do with **glimmer**.

shine

sing

save

sparkle

_____

_____

Teacher: Read aloud each numbered item. Have children read the word choices and write the two words that go with each vocabulary word. Ask children which words went with the vocabulary words and why.

2

Listen. Read. Draw.

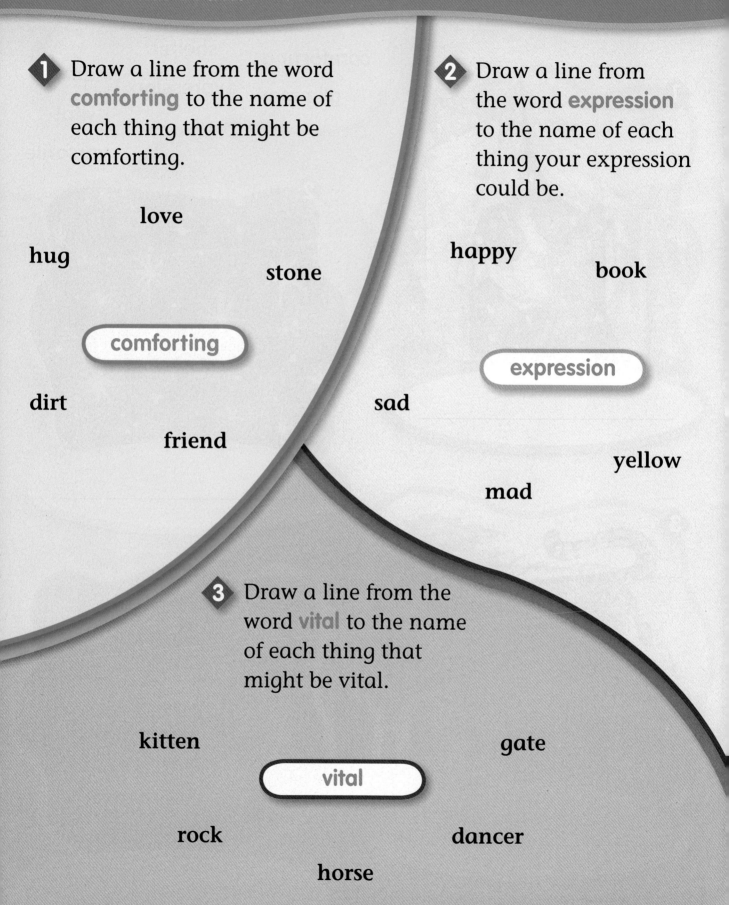

1 Draw a line from the word **comforting** to the name of each thing that might be comforting.

love

hug

stone

comforting

dirt

friend

2 Draw a line from the word **expression** to the name of each thing your expression could be.

happy

book

expression

sad

yellow

mad

3 Draw a line from the word **vital** to the name of each thing that might be vital.

kitten

gate

vital

rock

dancer

horse

Teacher: Read aloud each numbered item. Have children read the word choices and draw lines connecting each vocabulary word to the three words that go with it. Ask children which words they connected to the vocabulary words and why.

3

Listen. Write.

comforting shelter fleet
glimmer expression vital versatile

1

_____

2

_____

3

_____

4

_____

Teacher: Read aloud the vocabulary words. Have children look at each picture and write the vocabulary word that best describes it. Ask children which word they wrote under each picture and why.

4

1 What might someone who is **comforting** you say?
- ○ Please brush your teeth.
- ○ Everything will be all right.
- ○ Don't forget your homework.

2 What could you use to **shelter** yourself?
- ○ a mailbox
- ○ a rock
- ○ an umbrella

3 Which animal is **fleet**?
- ○ a racing horse
- ○ a barking dog
- ○ a sleeping cat

4 Which one **glimmers**?
- ○ a red shirt
- ○ a cloudy sky
- ○ a diamond ring

5 Which one is an **expression**?
- ○ a pencil
- ○ a smile
- ○ a nose

6 What might a **vital** person say?
- ○ I'm tired.
- ○ Let's have fun!
- ○ Please go away.

7 Which person is most **versatile**?
- ○ someone who can run very fast
- ○ someone who can write poems, ride a bike, and sing
- ○ someone who learns how to cook breakfast

1 "Why did you get pepperoni pizza?" asked Tony. "You know that I'm very **persnickety** about my pizza!"

persnickety

2 Mr. Romano won a contest. The prize was a dozen doughnuts. Mr. Romano was filled with **glee**.

glee

3 It was time for the big race. Jill and Janet had to **cooperate** if they wanted to win.

cooperate

Teacher: Read aloud each numbered item. Have children write the vocabulary word under the picture that shows its meaning. Ask children which picture they chose and why.

Listen. Read. Draw.

1 Draw a line from the word **weary** to other words that mean almost the same thing as weary.

tired

excited   sleepy

weary

awake

worn out

2 Draw a line from the word **murmur** to other words that mean about the same thing as murmur.

whisper   shout

yell   **murmur**

speak softly   mumble

3 Draw a line from the word **cooperate** to things that you can only do if you cooperate.

play baseball   play kickball

cooperate

watch TV   read a book

shake hands

Listen. Read. Write.

best

right   picky

blend

stir   exact   good

make

correct   mix   choosy

fussy

persnickety   proper   concoction

Teacher: Read aloud the vocabulary words that appear on the shelves. Have children read the words on the cans and write each word under its related vocabulary word. Ask children which words they wrote on each shelf and why.

1 Which shoes would be **proper** to wear to the beach?
- ○ warm boots
- ○ high-heeled shoes
- ○ summer sandals

2 Why would someone **murmur**?
- ○ so everyone can hear
- ○ so other people can barely hear
- ○ to talk to a large group of people

3 What might a **persnickety** eater do?
- ○ eat everything on the plate
- ○ ask for second helpings of everything
- ○ eat only one thing on the plate

4 What might make someone **weary**?
- ○ running a long race
- ○ opening presents
- ○ taking a nap

5 When might you feel **glee**?
- ○ winning a prize
- ○ losing a prize
- ○ breaking a prize

6 How can you **cooperate**?
- ○ by working alone
- ○ by working quickly
- ○ by working together

7 Which food could be a **concoction**?
- ○ a cracker
- ○ a banana split
- ○ a chicken leg

Listen. Read. Write.

1 Write the words that have to do with **details**.

big

parts

pieces

whole

_____

_____

2 Write the words that have to do with **perfect**.

_____

_____

best

right

wrong

worst

3 Write the words that have to do with **gallery**.

art

clock

game

painting

_____

_____

Teacher: Read aloud each numbered item. Have children read the word choices and write the two words that go with each vocabulary word. Ask children which words went with the vocabulary words and why.

Listen. Read. Draw.

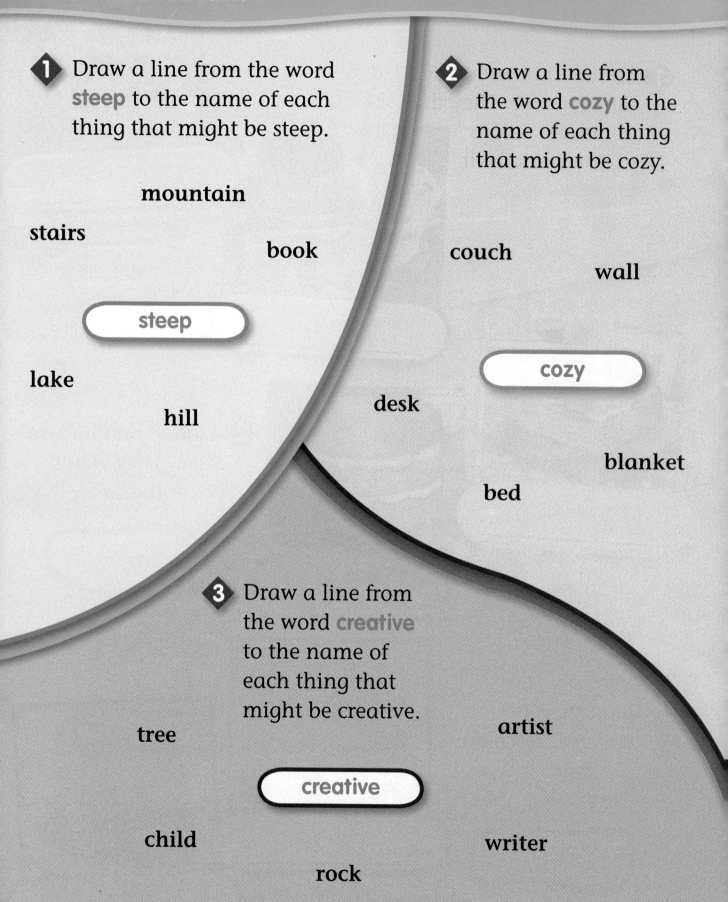

1 Draw a line from the word **steep** to the name of each thing that might be steep.

mountain

stairs

book

steep

lake

hill

2 Draw a line from the word **cozy** to the name of each thing that might be cozy.

couch

wall

cozy

desk

blanket

bed

3 Draw a line from the word **creative** to the name of each thing that might be creative.

tree

artist

creative

child

writer

rock

Teacher: Read aloud each numbered item. Have children read the word choices and draw lines connecting each vocabulary word to the three words that go with it. Ask children which words they connected to the vocabulary words and why.

11

Listen. Write.

1 Linda and her dad decided to make a cake. They thought about the **details** of how to make it.

_____

details

_____

_____

2 Linda's dad had an idea. They would **layer** the cake.

layer

_____

_____

3 The cake they made was **perfect**. It was a chocolate cake with lots of frosting.

perfect

_____

_____

Teacher: Read aloud each numbered item. Have children write the vocabulary word under the picture that shows its meaning. Ask children which picture they chose and why.

12

1 Which one is a **detail**?
- ○ a painting
- ○ a color used in a painting
- ○ a place with many paintings

2 Which homework would be **perfect**?
- ○ homework with no mistakes
- ○ messy homework
- ○ homework that is not finished

3 Which things would be hard to **layer**?
- ○ papers
- ○ clothes
- ○ balls

4 What could be **steep**?
- ○ a door
- ○ a stairway
- ○ a window

5 What might be a **cozy** place?
- ○ a soft bed
- ○ a wooden bench
- ○ a high chair

6 Which might be **creative**?
- ○ a sidewalk
- ○ a cloud
- ○ an idea

7 What might you see in a **gallery**?
- ○ animals
- ○ paintings
- ○ boats

Teacher: Read aloud each numbered item and have children fill in the bubble next to the correct answer.

13

prefer   coax

                crouch

feast   generous

                hectic

              dignified

1

2

_____

_____

3

4

_____

_____

Teacher: Read aloud the vocabulary words. Have children look at each picture and write the vocabulary word that best describes it. Ask children which word they wrote under each picture and why.

14

Listen. Read. Write.

1 Juan gave his little brother a **generous** helping of dinner. He knew that Tomás could eat a _____.

dish
lot
little

2 But Tomás **preferred** playing outside to eating his dinner. He thought that playing was _____ than eating.

worse
harder
better

3 Tomás wanted Juan to think that he was a **dignified** boy. So he used _____ manners and finished his dinner.

good
bad
poor

4 After dinner, Tomás **coaxed** Juan to come play with him. He _____ Juan to come to the park.

helped
begged
forced

5 Juan and Tomás went to the park, and it was so **hectic** there! They had never seen such a _____ place.

pretty
quiet
busy

Teacher: Read aloud each pair of sentences. Have children read the word choices and write the best word to fill in the blank. Ask children which words they chose and why.

15

1

One day the forest animals decided that they should have a picnic. The forest was _____ as the animals hurried to gather all of the foods they _____. The animals were _____, so there was plenty of food for everyone. The picnic had become a _____!

preferred

generous

feast

hectic

2

All of the animals came to the picnic. Squirrel even _____ Mole into leaving his hole. Everyone used good manners, but Mouse was the most _____ guest of all. When he saw some ants coming, he _____ down to welcome them to the picnic!

crouched

coaxed

dignified

Teacher: Read aloud the vocabulary words in the shapes. Then have children read each passage and write the best words to fill in the blanks. Ask children which words they chose to complete the story and why.

1 What might a **generous** boy do?
- ○ share his lunch
- ○ buy his lunch
- ○ bring his lunch

2 Which meal would be a **feast**?
- ○ a peanut butter sandwich and a piece of fruit
- ○ a bowl of spaghetti, three vegetables, and dessert
- ○ a bowl of cereal and a glass of juice

3 Which one might a **dignified** person say?
- ○ Get over here.
- ○ Give me that.
- ○ Thank you very much.

4 Which place would be **hectic**?
- ○ a quiet garden
- ○ a busy airport
- ○ a country road

5 Which would you say if you were **coaxing** someone?
- ○ It's too late to go now.
- ○ I'll just go by myself.
- ○ It will be more fun if you come, too.

6 What do you bend when you **crouch**?
- ○ your fingers
- ○ your knees
- ○ your neck

7 If you were telling what you **prefer**, what might you say?
- ○ I like red shoes better than black ones.
- ○ I have some blue shoes at home.
- ○ I am wearing my white shoes today.

1

Prevail

Faithful

Pledge

A _____ Friend

Taylor had a bad day at school. But as soon as she got home, her dog, Scooter, was there to cheer her up. Taylor gave Scooter a big hug and felt her worries melting away. She knew her friend would always be there for her.

2

A _____ to Do Better

Taylor decided to make tomorrow a better day. She promised to try her best. She wouldn't forget her homework or her lunch. Taylor said, "Scooter, I am going to have a good day tomorrow, and that is that!"

3

Taylor Will _____!

The next morning Taylor made sure she had everything she needed for school. She was ready for a new day. "Scooter," she said, "I'm going to have a GREAT day today!"

18 **Teacher:** Read aloud the vocabulary words at the top of the page. Have children read the stories and write a vocabulary word to complete each title. Ask children which words they chose to complete the titles and why.

Listen. Read. Write.

1 James was determined to **prevail**. Even though he was tired, he tried his best to _____ the bike race.

win
lose
like

2 Tessa told her dad, "I **pledge** to read for at least one hour every day." Tessa made a _____ to her dad.

joke
promise
face

3 When the daisy opened, its petals **radiated**. They looked like they were stretching out from the flower's _____.

center
leaf
sides

4 Lee was **confident** she would win first place in the contest. She knew it would happen the way she _____ it to.

asked
disliked
wanted

5 The kitten was **faithful** to the old cat. No matter what the old cat did, the kitten still _____ her.

loved
bothered
teased

Listen. Read. Write.

1

One dark morning the sun felt much too _____ to shine. It hid behind the hills and would not come up. Rooster promised to help the sun. He said, "I _____ to bring the sun out of its hiding place. I am _____ that I will _____!"

pledge
humble
prevail
confident

2

Rooster started to crow, and as he did the sun started to laugh. As the sun laughed, it rose higher and higher in the sky. Soon its light _____ all around. Rooster and the sun became _____ friends. Now every morning Rooster crows for the sun, and the sun never _____ coming out to shine.

faithful
overlooks
radiated

"cockadoodle doo!"

Teacher: Read aloud the vocabulary words in the shapes. Then have children read each passage and write the best words to fill in the blanks. Ask children which words they chose to complete the story and why.

1 Who might be **humble**?
- ○ a boy who loves attention
- ○ a boy who is shy
- ○ a boy who shows off

2 Who might be **confident**?
- ○ a girl who always quits
- ○ a girl who always tries her best
- ○ a girl who never tries anything

3 Who would be **faithful** to each other?
- ○ a parent and child
- ○ two strangers
- ○ two enemies

4 Which one can **radiate**?
- ○ a baseball
- ○ a rock
- ○ the sun

5 Why would someone make a **pledge**?
- ○ to promise something
- ○ to ask for something
- ○ to buy something

6 Which person **prevails** in a race?
- ○ the person who loses
- ○ the person who comes in second
- ○ the person who wins

7 If you **overlook** something, what do you do?
- ○ You pick it up.
- ○ You don't notice it.
- ○ You look right at it.

1 Lani and her grandfather went to the zoo. "Look!" said her grandfather. "That animal is **fierce**!"

_____

fierce

_____

_____

_____

2 Mike's mom has many tools. She can **repair** almost anything.

repair

3 Olivia looked up to her big sister. She always asked her for **advice**.

_____

advice

_____

Teacher: Read aloud each numbered item. Have children write the vocabulary word under the picture that shows its meaning. Ask children which picture they chose and why.

22

Listen. Read. Write.

1 Write the words that have to do with **ruin**.

mend

rip

break

fix

_____

_____

2 Write the words that have to do with **disaster**.

_____

_____

mess

moon

trouble

trip

3 Write the words that have to do with **perspective**.

run

look

sleep

see

_____

_____

Listen. Read. Write.

mean

light

talk

wild

teach

angry

coach

white

scary

pink

help

gray

fierce

_____

_____

_____

_____

pale

_____

_____

_____

_____

advice

_____

_____

_____

_____

Teacher: Read aloud the vocabulary words that appear on each plate. Have children read the words on the tortillas and write each word under its related vocabulary word. Ask children which words they wrote on each plate and why.

1 What might be a **disaster**?
- ○ finding ten cents
- ○ dropping your pencil
- ○ crashing your bike

2 Which could be **repaired**?
- ○ a broken fence
- ○ a dead tree
- ○ a burned log

3 What might be your dentist's **advice**?
- ○ Eat lots of candy.
- ○ Drink more sodas.
- ○ Brush your teeth every day.

4 Which is a **pale** color?
- ○ dark red
- ○ light green
- ○ bright blue

5 Which is a **fierce** animal?
- ○ a tiger
- ○ a chicken
- ○ a puppy

6 How might you **ruin** a surprise party?
- ○ by keeping it a secret
- ○ by going to the party
- ○ by telling everyone about it

7 Who might have the same **perspective** on homework?
- ○ a baby and a grandfather
- ○ a teacher and a principal
- ○ a parent and a dog

1 Dan and Sara are friends who like to **compete** with each other.

compete

2 Dan and Sara decided to find out who could read the most. They had fun choosing from the **assorted** books.

assorted

3 Ms. Jackson got even more books from the closet. Then she **latched** the door.

Teacher: Read aloud each numbered item. Have children write the vocabulary word under the picture that shows its meaning. Ask children which picture they chose and why.

Listen. Read. Write.

1

We **defeated** the other kickball team. We
_____ the game!

won

hated

lost

2

My cats are often in **combat**. They always
_____ with each other.

walk

play

fight

3

Sean was in a real **predicament**. He had
a big _____.

parade

problem

secret

4

Tyler's sister **clings** to him. She grabs his
hand and won't _____.

cry

let go

talk

5

Kayla **latched** the gate. She wanted to
be sure it stayed _____.

open

painted

closed

Teacher: Read aloud each pair of sentences. Have children read the word choices and write the
best word to fill in the blank. Ask children which words they chose and why.

Listen. Read. Write.

Compete

Predicament

Assorted

1

Paul's _____

Paul the penguin had a big problem. He was hurrying because he was running late, and he did not look where he was going. Crash! Paul ran right into a snow-cone cart. Now Paul was a mess—and he was still late!

2

The _____ Marbles

Laura had a big bag of marbles. Every marble was different. Laura played with her marbles all the time. She loved playing with marbles of every size and color.

3

Katya Can _____!

Katya the koala loved contests. She entered them all. She entered the tree-climbing contest. She entered the leaf-gathering contest. She even entered the koala races. Katya always kept trying until she won. She wanted to be the best at everything.

Teacher: Read aloud the vocabulary words at the top of the page. Have children read the stories and write a vocabulary word to complete each title. Ask children which words they chose to complete the titles and why.

1 Which one can be **latched**?
- ○ a door
- ○ a chair
- ○ a bed

2 Which friends are **competing**?
- ○ two friends watching TV
- ○ two friends eating lunch
- ○ two friends playing tug-of-war

3 Which prince is in **combat**?
- ○ a prince fighting a dragon
- ○ a prince marrying a princess
- ○ a prince turning into a frog

4 Which candies are **assorted**?
- ○ candies that are all the same color
- ○ candies that are different sizes and colors
- ○ candies that are all the same size

5 Which child is **clinging**?
- ○ a scared child holding onto her mother
- ○ a happy child laughing with her mother
- ○ a hungry child eating with her mother

6 Which team was **defeated**?
- ○ the best team
- ○ the winning team
- ○ the losing team

7 Which kitten is in a **predicament**?
- ○ a kitten chasing a ball
- ○ a kitten stuck in a tree
- ○ a kitten taking a nap

Teacher: Read aloud each numbered item and have children fill in the bubble next to the correct answer.

plead

compassion

infest

treacherous

groom

discover

exceptional

_____

_____

_____

_____

Teacher: Read aloud the vocabulary words. Have children look at each picture and write the vocabulary word that best describes it. Ask children which word they wrote under each picture and why.

groom
discovered
infested
pleaded

1 Megan heard something squeaking. Outside she _____ a little kitten. Megan's mom said, "That kitten is _____ with fleas!" Megan _____ with her mother to keep the kitten. She said, "Please, Mom! I promise that I will _____ her so she stays nice and clean."

exceptional
compassion
treacherous

2 Megan's mom said, "Outdoors can be a _____ place for a little kitten." She showed _____ for the kitten and let Megan keep her. The kitten grew up to be very smart and talented. She was an _____ cat!

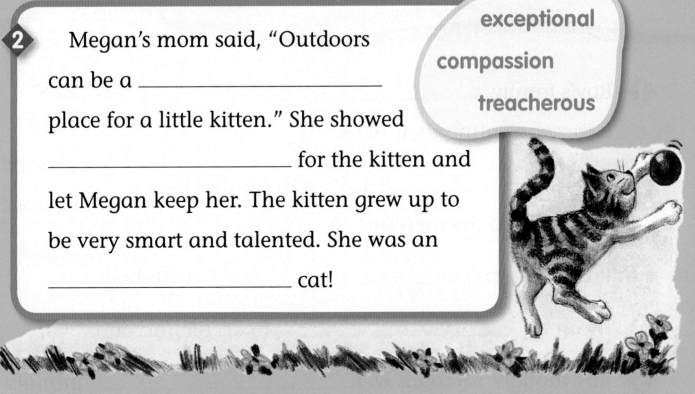

Teacher: Read aloud the vocabulary words in the shapes. Then have children read each passage and write the best words to fill in the blanks. Ask children which words they chose to complete the story and why.

31

Read. Listen. Write.

Roy and his family went camping. One night, they were surprised to find a raccoon eating their food. Roy begged his dad to let him keep it as a pet.

Roy's dad explained that raccoons can have lots of bugs on them and can sometimes be dangerous to people. Roy decided to watch the raccoon from his tent instead. He was amazed at how smart raccoons could be!

infested

exceptional

pleaded

discovered

treacherous

1 Roy's family _____ a raccoon eating their food.

2 Roy _____ with his dad to let him keep the raccoon.

3 Raccoons can be _____ with bugs.

4 It can be _____ to keep a raccoon.

5 Roy thought raccoons were _____ animals.

Teacher: Have children read the story. Then read the vocabulary words aloud. Have children read the sentences and write the vocabulary word that best completes each sentence. Ask children which words they wrote and why.

1 What might a person who **pleads** say?
- ○ Don't do that!
- ○ Please help us!
- ○ Dinner is ready!

2 What does an **infested** animal have on it?
- ○ dirt
- ○ water
- ○ bugs

3 When you **groom** a dog, what do you do?
- ○ give it a bath
- ○ take it for a walk
- ○ teach it a trick

4 What might you say when you **discover** something?
- ○ I already knew that.
- ○ I don't think so.
- ○ I didn't know that before.

5 What might a person with **compassion** say?
- ○ Let me help you.
- ○ I don't care.
- ○ Leave me alone!

6 Which dog would be **exceptional**?
- ○ a dog that can run
- ○ a dog that can bark
- ○ a dog that can sing

7 Which place is probably **treacherous**?
- ○ a fluffy bed
- ○ a high cliff
- ○ a grassy field

Teacher: Read aloud each numbered item and have children fill in the bubble next to the correct answer.

33

1 Draw a line from the word **lure** to the name of each thing that might lure a bird.

seeds

cat   truck

lure

worm

nest

2 Draw a line from the word **sketch** to the name of each thing that you might use to sketch.

pen

comb

sketch

paper   pencil

toothbrush

3 Draw a line from the word **stern** to each item that means almost the same thing as stern.

happy   stern   friendly

serious   mean

unfriendly

Teacher: Read aloud each numbered item. Have children read the word choices and draw lines connecting each vocabulary word to the three words that go with it. Ask children which words they connected to the vocabulary words and why.

34

Listen. Write.

sketch flustered

stern

precise lure

sensational

chaos

1

2

3

4

Teacher: Read aloud the vocabulary words. Have children look at each picture and write the vocabulary word that best describes it. Ask children which word they wrote under each picture and why.

35

Listen. Read. Write.

1 Nick was **flustered** because he could not find his backpack. His dad could tell that Nick was _____.

upset
happy
calm

2 "You need stitches," Dr. Romano said in a **stern** voice. Daniel had never heard the doctor sound so _____.

silly
serious
funny

3 Maria was **precise** as she fixed the parts of the watch. She was _____ with each thing she did.

messy
careless
careful

4 There was **chaos** on the field when the Hawks won the football game. The crowd went _____.

quiet
still
wild

5 Sarah watched as the acrobats did one **sensational** trick after another. She thought the circus was _____.

exciting
boring
ordinary

Teacher: Read aloud each pair of sentences. Have children read the word choices and write the best word to fill in the blank. Ask children which words they chose and why.

1 What would a person who is **sketching** do?
- ○ make a quick drawing
- ○ read a long book
- ○ paint a colorful painting

2 What might make someone **flustered**?
- ○ singing a song
- ○ dropping a pile of papers
- ○ watching TV

3 How might a person who is **stern** look?
- ○ serious
- ○ puzzled
- ○ sleepy

4 What would help you be **precise**?
- ○ a bike
- ○ a car
- ○ a ruler

5 How would you **lure** a mouse?
- ○ with a trap
- ○ with a cat
- ○ with a piece of cheese

6 What might you hear if your class is in **chaos**?
- ○ silence
- ○ loud noise
- ○ raindrops

7 What would be **sensational**?
- ○ eating cereal for breakfast
- ○ drinking milk at dinner
- ○ eating spaghetti that can change colors

Teacher: Read aloud each numbered item and have children fill in the bubble next to the correct answer.

37

Listen. Read. Write.

different

lost

change

confuse

mix up

problem

answer

solve

turn into

transform

bewilder

solution

_____

_____

_____

_____

_____

_____

_____

_____

_____

Teacher: Read aloud the vocabulary words that appear on each boulder. Have children read the words on the fence and write each word under its related vocabulary word. Ask children which words they wrote on each

Miki was trying to guess the answer to a riddle. She tried and tried, but she could not think of the answer. The riddle made her very confused. She jumped up and down, but that didn't help. She ran around in circles. Then she stood on her head.

Miki tried and tried some more. She thought she saw the answer outside, but she knew it was not real. She looked up at the bright, shining stars. Miki wished the stars above would change into the answer to the riddle!

bewildered

transform

solution

illusion

brilliant

1 Miki tried many ways to find the

_____ to the riddle.

2 The riddle _____ Miki.

3 Miki thought she saw the answer outside, but it

was an _____.

4 The stars above looked _____.

5 Miki wished the stars would _____ into

the answer.

Teacher: Have children read the story. Then read the vocabulary words aloud. Have children read the sentences and write the vocabulary word that best completes each sentence. Ask children which words they wrote and why.

Listen. Read. Write.

1

The _____ Butterfly

The flowers in the garden loved to watch the butterflies that came to visit them. The butterfly named Flora was very brightly colored. Flora's wings looked like a rainbow!

2

The _____ Butterfly

Sunny was a very bright butterfly. He was even brighter than the sun! On cloudy days, Sunny came to the garden to shine light on the flowers.

3

The _____ Butterfly

All of the flowers giggled when Bella the butterfly flew by, but Bella didn't care. She loved her silly sunglasses. She liked looking different from all of the other butterflies.

Teacher: Read aloud the vocabulary words at the top of the page. Have children read the stories and write a vocabulary word to complete each title. Ask children which words they chose to complete the titles and why.

40

1 What color is **vivid**?
- ○ gray
- ○ red
- ○ white

2 Which would be an **illusion**?
- ○ a piece of fruit
- ○ plastic fruit that looks real
- ○ an empty fruit bowl

3 Which might be **brilliant**?
- ○ raindrops
- ○ mud puddle
- ○ sunshine

4 Which hat might be **quirky**?
- ○ a hat with a propeller on top
- ○ a baseball cap
- ○ a cowboy hat

5 Which insect **transforms**?
- ○ a caterpillar
- ○ an ant
- ○ a bee

6 Which might **bewilder** you?
- ○ turning on the TV
- ○ eating cereal
- ○ figuring out a secret code

7 When would you need a **solution**?
- ○ when you are brushing your teeth
- ○ when you have a problem
- ○ when you are combing your hair

exaggerate   motivate

overcome   wistful   moist

crumble

edge

Teacher: Read aloud the vocabulary words. Have children look at each picture and write the vocabulary word that best describes it. Ask children which word they wrote under each picture and why.

Listen. Read. Write.

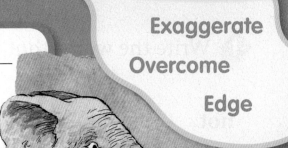
1

A Problem to _____

   Marta's class was going to the zoo, but Marta had a problem. She was afraid of elephants. Marta decided to fix her problem. She learned all about elephants. Soon she knew that elephants were nothing to be afraid of!

2

Jack Likes to _____

   Jack always tells tall tales. He starts with something real, but the stories get bigger and bigger. Jack's favorite story is about a mouse. "You've never seen a mouse like this," he says. "It was as big as a dog!"

3

A Hike to the _____

   Kylie loves to hike. She can walk along the trails for hours. One time Kylie's family hiked to the top of a cliff and looked down. From the end of the trail, they could see everything below!

Teacher: Read aloud the vocabulary words at the top of the page. Have children read the stories and write a vocabulary word to complete each title. Ask children which words they chose to complete the titles and why.

Listen. Read. Write.

1 Write the words that have to do with **moist**.

hot

splash

wet

book

_____

_____

2 Write the words that have to do with **wistful**.

_____

_____

remember

laugh

excited

unhappy

3 Write the words that have to do with **crumble**.

rope

cookie

break

mud

_____

_____

Teacher: Read aloud each numbered item. Have children read the word choices and write the two words that go with each vocabulary word. Ask children which words went with the vocabulary words and why.

44

1 Which could you **crumble**?
- ○ a heavy rock
- ○ a dry cracker
- ○ a shiny nickel

2 Where is the **edge** of a lake?
- ○ around the outside
- ○ in the middle
- ○ under the water

3 Which would be **moist**?
- ○ a flower that was sprinkled with water
- ○ a soaking wet swimsuit
- ○ a blanket left outside in the hot sun

4 When might someone feel **wistful**?
- ○ winning a blue ribbon
- ○ remembering an old friend
- ○ finding five dollars

5 Which might someone want to **overcome**?
- ○ a fear of spiders
- ○ a favorite place
- ○ a friend's house

6 Which sentence is **exaggerating**?
- ○ That building is tall.
- ○ That building is 100 miles high.
- ○ That building is very big.

7 What might someone say to **motivate** a friend?
- ○ You'll never learn how to do that!
- ○ I'm going home right now!
- ○ I know you can do it!

1 Write the words that have to do with **innovative**.

lazy

idea   different

repeat

_____

_____

2 Write the words that have to do with **refreshing**.

_____

_____

blanket

cool

splash

warm

3 Write the words that have to do with **elegant**.

fancy

broken

dull

pretty

_____

_____

Teacher: Read aloud each numbered item. Have children read the word choices and write the two words that go with each vocabulary word. Ask children which words went with the vocabulary words and why.

Listen. Write.

1

_____

2

_____

3

_____

4

_____

Teacher: Read aloud the vocabulary words. Have children look at each picture and write the vocabulary word that best describes it. Ask children which word they wrote under each picture and why.

47

Listen. Read. Write.

swelter

satisfied

innovative

smiling

heat

happy

new

pleased

weather

summer

clever

different

Teacher: Read aloud the vocabulary words that appear on each pitcher. Have children read the words on the stones and write each word under its related vocabulary word. Ask children which words they wrote on each pitcher and why.

1 Which would be elegant?
- ○ a pair of ripped jeans
- ○ a dirty shirt
- ○ a pretty dress

2 Which might make someone swelter?
- ○ wearing a heavy coat in the summer
- ○ eating ice cream in the summer
- ○ going swimming in the winter

3 Which might be an obstacle in a race?
- ○ people cheering from the sides
- ○ birds flying high in the sky
- ○ sticks lying on the track

4 What would a hungry mouse find tempting?
- ○ a large cat
- ○ a piece of cheese
- ○ a place to sleep

5 Which might be refreshing after a soccer game?
- ○ drinking a glass of ice water
- ○ taking a hot bath
- ○ drinking a mug of warm tea

6 Which sentence describes something innovative?
- ○ I have that same toy at home!
- ○ I've never seen anything like that before!
- ○ That has been done a million times before!

7 Which would make a student feel satisfied?
- ○ getting more homework
- ○ starting a math paper
- ○ doing well on a test

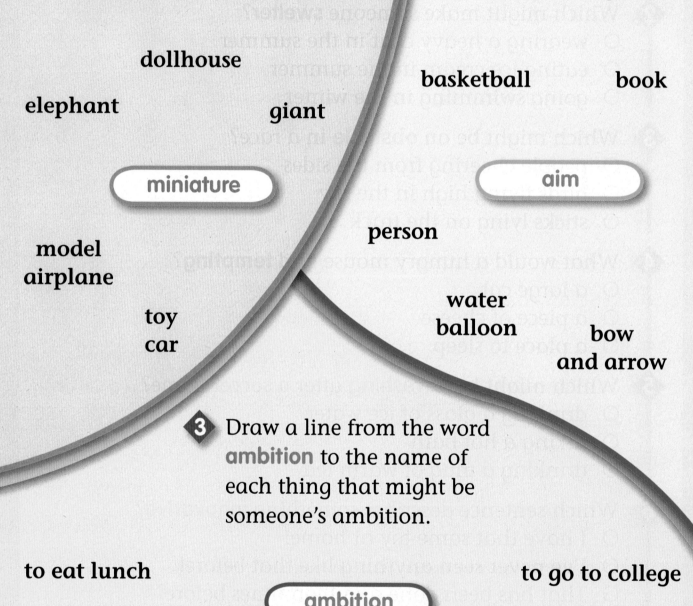

1 Draw a line from the word **miniature** to the name of each thing that might be miniature.

dollhouse

elephant   giant

miniature

model airplane

toy car

2 Draw a line from the word **aim** to the name of each thing that you might aim.

basketball   book

aim

person

water balloon

bow and arrow

3 Draw a line from the word **ambition** to the name of each thing that might be someone's ambition.

to eat lunch   to go to college

ambition

to be a doctor   to go home

to be the best

Teacher: Read aloud each numbered item. Have children read the word choices and draw lines connecting each vocabulary word to the three words that go with it. Ask children which words they connected to the vocabulary words and why.

Listen. Write.

miniature   scan

aim   prance   ambition   retrieve

assume

1

_____

2

_____

3

_____

4

_____

Teacher: Read aloud the vocabulary words. Have
children look at each picture and write the vocabulary word
that best describes it. Ask children which word they wrote under each picture and why.

51

My uncle took me to a horse show. He quickly looked around and spotted our two seats. I thought the horses would just run around the ring. But when the horses came out, they moved all around with high, quick steps. They even did tricks.

For one of the tricks, the horse trainer hid a wagon behind some hay. Her horse walked around until it found the wagon. It pulled the wagon back to the trainer. It was a good trick! After the show ended, I said to my uncle, "I want to be a horse trainer when I grow up!"

1 The uncle had to _____ to find their seats.

2 The girl _____ the horses would run in circles.

3 The horses _____ all around.

4 One horse _____ a wagon.

5 It was the girl's _____ to become a horse trainer.

assumed

ambition

scan

retrieved

pranced

Teacher: Have children read the story. Then read the vocabulary words aloud. Have children read the sentences and write the vocabulary word that best completes each sentence. Ask children which words they wrote and why.

1 If you **scan**, how would your eyes move?
   ○ slowly
   ○ up and down
   ○ quickly

2 If you **prance**, how would your knees move?
   ○ up high
   ○ in circles
   ○ not at all

3 If you **aim** a paper airplane, what would you be doing?
   ○ dropping it
   ○ pointing it
   ○ throwing it

4 If you had a **miniature** doll, how big would it be?
   ○ tiny
   ○ normal sized
   ○ very large

5 If you have **ambition**, what might you want?
   ○ to get some sleep
   ○ to do great things one day
   ○ to get something to eat

6 If you **retrieve** something, what might you say?
   ○ I found it!
   ○ Get away from me!
   ○ It's gone forever!

7 If you **assume** you are late, what might you say?
   ○ I see by the time on the clock that I am late.
   ○ I don't care if I am late or not.
   ○ I don't know what time it is, but I think that I'm late.

Teacher: Read aloud each numbered item and have children fill in the bubble next to the correct answer.

53

Listen. Write.

1 There is a statue of Mr. Smith in front of the library. At the bottom of the statue, there is a special **inscription**.

inscription

2 Tran found a dog with a cut paw. Tran always treated animals in a **humane** way.

humane

3 Tina noticed a woman in the store carrying two bags. Tina was **gracious** to the woman as she left the store.

gracious

Teacher: Read aloud each numbered item. Have children write the vocabulary word under the picture that shows its meaning. Ask children which picture they chose and why.

Listen. Read. Write.

1 The **diplomat** shook hands with the president. She hoped they could work together to _____ their problems.

make
solve
read

2 "I heard that you are making a new movie," said the reporter. "Can you **confirm** that it is _____?"

true
wrong
false

3 The new student asked me to **indicate** where the office was. I _____ her where it was and how to get there.

cut
showed
threw

4 The boy was **gracious** when his grandmother gave him dinner. He _____ said, "Thank you."

rudely
loudly
nicely

5 Tomas **declared**, "I have something very _____ to say. Wash your hands before eating!"

quiet
important
silly

Teacher: Read aloud each pair of sentences. Have children read the word choices and write the best word to fill in the blank. Ask children which words they chose and why.

55

Listen. Read. Write.

1   Benjamin Franklin did many different things. He _____ that "A penny saved is a penny earned." He helped our country solve problems as a _____ to France. He had good manners and was known as a _____ man. He was also _____ to animals.

gracious

humane

declared

diplomat

2   If you go to Washington, D.C., you can see a statue of Benjamin Franklin. Someone there can _____ it to you. There is an _____ carved into both sides of the statue. You can read a book about Benjamin Franklin to _____ that these things are true.

confirm

inscription

indicate

Teacher: Read aloud the vocabulary words in the shapes. Then have children read each passage and write the best words to fill in the blanks. Ask children which words they chose to complete each story and why.

1 How could you **indicate** something?
   ○ run away
   ○ shrug your shoulders
   ○ point your finger

2 What might you say to **confirm** something?
   ○ That is not true.
   ○ I am guessing.
   ○ I can show you that it is true.

3 What kind of voice would you use to **declare** something?
   ○ a quiet voice
   ○ a loud voice
   ○ a sad voice

4 Which is a **gracious** thing to say?
   ○ Get out of my way!
   ○ I can't help you!
   ○ I'm very pleased to meet you.

5 What would a **humane** person do?
   ○ be nice to a sad person
   ○ stay away from other people
   ○ say mean things about a person

6 Where might a **diplomat** work?
   ○ at a school
   ○ at a swimming pool
   ○ in other countries

7 Where might you see an **inscription**?
   ○ on a metal tag
   ○ on a scrap of paper
   ○ in the sky

1

The _____ Flute Player

Tametra played the flute better than anyone else. Many people came to see her concerts. Tametra loved playing her flute and was happy she could share her music with so many people.

2

The _____ Flute Player

Annie was going to play her flute in a big concert, but she was worried. What if she made a mistake? Would people laugh at her? When it was her turn to play, Annie was scared, but she played well. She didn't make a single mistake.

3

The _____ Flute Player

Monica played the flute in a band. One day she saw someone steal a tuba. Monica told her teacher what she had seen, and the teacher got the tuba back. Monica was glad that she had done the right thing.

Teacher: Read aloud the vocabulary words at the top of the page. Have children read the stories and write a vocabulary word to complete each title. Ask children which words they chose to complete the titles and why.

Listen. Read. Draw.

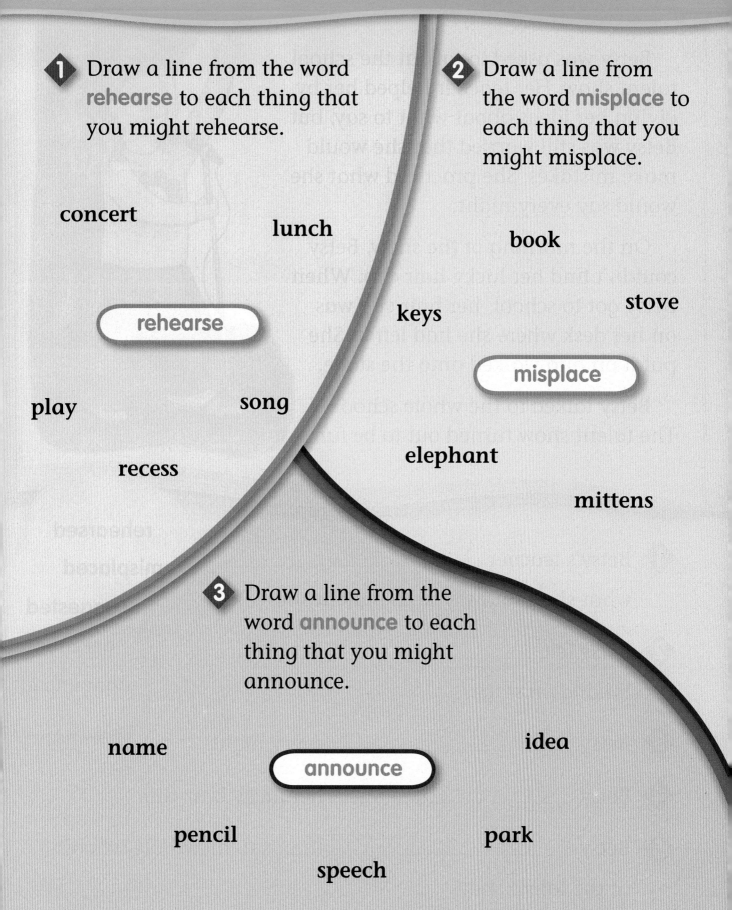

1 Draw a line from the word **rehearse** to each thing that you might rehearse.

concert

lunch

rehearse

play

song

recess

2 Draw a line from the word **misplace** to each thing that you might misplace.

book

stove

keys

misplace

elephant

mittens

3 Draw a line from the word **announce** to each thing that you might announce.

name

idea

announce

pencil

park

speech

Teacher: Read aloud each numbered item. Have children read the word choices and draw lines connecting each vocabulary word to the three words that go with it. Ask children which words they connected to the vocabulary words and why.

Betsy was asked to talk at the school talent show. Her teacher helped her by giving her ideas about what to say, but Betsy was still worried that she would make mistakes. She practiced what she would say every night.

On the morning of the show, Betsy couldn't find her lucky hair clip. When Betsy got to school, her hair clip was on her desk where she had left it. She put it on and walked onto the stage.

Betsy talked to the whole school. The talent show turned out to be fun.

1 Betsy's teacher _____ what she could say at the talent show.

2 Betsy felt _____ about talking on stage.

3 Betsy _____ every night.

4 Betsy _____ her lucky hair clip.

5 Betsy _____ things to the whole school at the talent show.

rehearsed
misplaced
suggested
nervous
announced

Teacher: Have children read the story. Then read the vocabulary words aloud. Have children read the sentences and write the vocabulary word that best completes each sentence. Ask children which words they wrote and why.

60

1 If you were **nervous**, how might you feel?
- ○ shaky
- ○ calm
- ○ sleepy

2 If you were **announcing** something, what might you say?
- ○ What is your name?
- ○ Hello, everyone. Welcome to my home!
- ○ I'd like to tell you a secret.

3 If you were **rehearsing**, what might you do?
- ○ sit quietly and watch others
- ○ clap when the music ends
- ○ practice something over and over

4 If you were **famous**, what might you say?
- ○ No one knows me.
- ○ My picture is on a magazine cover!
- ○ Only my friends know my name.

5 If you were **honorable**, what might people say to you?
- ○ Who are you?
- ○ You did a great thing.
- ○ What you did was wrong.

6 If you were **suggesting**, what might you say?
- ○ I have an idea you might like.
- ○ I don't know what you're talking about.
- ○ Thank you very much.

7 Which is something that you might **misplace**?
- ○ a house
- ○ a library book
- ○ a desk

fraction   convince

    contribute   motion

courtesy   humorous

         host

1

_____

2

_____

3

_____

4

_____

Teacher: Read aloud the vocabulary words. Have children look at each picture and write the vocabulary word that best describes it. Ask children which word they wrote under each picture and why.

Listen. Read. Write.

1. I told Robbie, "I want to **contribute** something to your snack. Can I _____ you some peanut butter for your apple?"

give
take
lend

2. "Peanut butter on an apple is a **humorous** snack," said Robbie. "I hope you were just being _____."

sad
mean
funny

3. "It's a great snack," I said. "When Maria **hosted** a _____, she served us apple slices with peanut butter."

school
party
parade

4. "I was just showing **courtesy** and being _____ to Maria by tasting one. But then I really liked it!"

loud
polite
silly

5. "You **convinced** me," Robbie said. "I will _____ your strange snack."

taste
hate
smell

Teacher: Read aloud each pair of sentences. Have children read the word choices and write the best word to fill in the blank. Ask children which words they chose and why.

Listen. Read. Write.

prove

part

beg

help

piece

aid

talk

half

give

offer

ask

some

convince

fraction

contribute

Teacher: Read aloud the vocabulary words on each tray. Have children read the words on the cups and write each word under its related vocabulary word. Ask children which words they wrote on each tray and why.

1 Which is something that might be a **fraction**?
- O a banana
- O a piece of pizza
- O an empty plate

2 Which one would be **motioning**?
- O a sneeze
- O a hand signal
- O a sleeping dog

3 Which is something you can **contribute**?
- O your help
- O a firefighter
- O a forest

4 Which person is **hosting**?
- O someone eating in a resturant
- O a guest staying with you
- O a person throwing a party

5 Which is something that might be **humorous**?
- O a flood
- O a clown
- O a sick friend

6 Which shows **courtesy**?
- O thanking someone
- O frowning at someone
- O yelling at someone

7 Which would you say to **convince** someone?
- O Thank you for coming over.
- O You must do as I say.
- O Please go with me. It will be fun.

Teacher: Read aloud each numbered item and have children fill in the bubble next to the correct answer.

65

exclaim handsome
rare ridiculous
succulent
opportunity
command

1

_____

2

_____

3

_____

4

WOW!

_____

Teacher: Read aloud the vocabulary words. Have
children look at each picture and write the vocabulary
word that best describes it. Ask children which word
they wrote under each picture and why.

Listen. Read. Write.

1 The **succulent** fruit tasted great. But it

_____ on Jenny's dress.

fell
dripped
rolled

2 This is a great **opportunity** for Nell. She loves
to do _____ things.

dull
hard
new

3 Tom found a **rare** penny in the street. There
are _____ others like it.

few
many
fifty

4 My brother is so **handsome**. People always
say he looks _____.

nice
clean
ugly

5 The policeman **commanded** the man to stop.
He used a _____ voice.

quiet
funny
strong

Teacher: Read aloud each pair of sentences. Have children read the word choices and write
the best word to fill in the blank. Ask children which words they chose and why.

67

Listen. Read. Write.

1   Katie, Billy, and Matt went to a costume party. They each had an

_____ to win a prize for having the best costume. Katie dressed as a cat. Billy dressed as a _____ prince. Matt wore a silly hat covered with _____ fruit.

handsome

succulent

opportunity

2   "You look so funny, Matt!"

_____ Katie. "Where did you find that _____ hat? I _____ you to tell me where you got it!"

   Matt won a prize for having such a _____ costume. Nobody had ever seen a hat like his before!

command

rare   exclaimed

ridiculous

68

Teacher: Read aloud the vocabulary words in the shapes. Then have children read each passage and write the best words to fill in the blanks. Ask children which words they chose to complete the story and why.

1 Which one might you **exclaim**?
- ○ I love to sing.
- ○ My coat is warm.
- ○ Ouch!

2 How does something **succulent** taste?
- ○ bad
- ○ juicy
- ○ dry

3 How often might you see something **rare**?
- ○ every day
- ○ all the time
- ○ once a year

4 What might you have an **opportunity** to do?
- ○ see something special
- ○ go home
- ○ write your name

5 What would you do if you saw something **ridiculous**?
- ○ laugh
- ○ cry
- ○ eat

6 What might you wear to look more **handsome**?
- ○ your ripped clothes
- ○ your old clothes
- ○ your best clothes

7 Which words would you use to **command** someone?
- ○ I'm tired!
- ○ Stop right there!
- ○ You are funny!

1 Tim's mom has many tools. She is always _____ to help Tim fix his bike and toys. She even _____ his clothes. Tim is _____ that his mom is always there to help him. He feels lucky to have a _____ mom.

dependable
grateful
mends
prepared

2 One day Tim _____ over the fence and saw a cat sneaking up on a bird. He knew that cats can be very _____ when they hunt. Tim wanted to help the bird. He made a loud noise. The bird _____ and flew away!

shrieked
sly
peered

Teacher: Read aloud the vocabulary words in the shapes. Then have children read each passage and write the best words to fill in the blanks. Ask children which words they chose to complete each story and why.

Listen. Read. Write.

fix

sneaky

shout

smart

scream

clever

sew

paste

tape

yell

cry

tricky

mend

shriek

sly

Teacher: Read aloud the vocabulary words that appear on each dresser. Have children read the words on the shirts and write each word under its related vocabulary word. Ask children which words they wrote on each dresser and why.

71

Kim loves going to school. She gets there early every morning to help her teacher get ready.

One morning Kim looked carefully at all of the books and found the ones that needed to be fixed. Her teacher thanked her for doing a good job that day!

While Kim was busy, her friend Mike tiptoed up behind her and tapped Kim on her arm. Kim was so surprised she yelled out loud!

grateful

sly

shrieked

peered

prepare

1 Kim helps her teacher _____ every day.

2 Kim _____ at the books.

3 Kim's teacher felt _____ to Kim for helping.

4 Mike was acting _____ when he came up behind Kim.

5 Kim _____ when Mike tapped her arm.

Teacher: Have children read the story. Then read the vocabulary words aloud. Have children read the sentences and write the vocabulary word that best completes each sentence. Ask children which words they wrote and why.

1 If someone **shrieked**, what would you hear?
- ○ a loud scream
- ○ a soft laugh
- ○ a low whistle

2 If you are **prepared** to go camping, what are you?
- ○ late
- ○ ready
- ○ hungry

3 If someone is **dependable**, what might they do?
- ○ help you sometimes
- ○ never help you
- ○ help you all the time

4 What would a **sly** person do?
- ○ trick someone
- ○ shout about something
- ○ find what someone lost

5 What might make you feel **grateful**?
- ○ if a friend wins a game you are playing
- ○ if a friend helps you do something
- ○ if a friend can't come out to play

6 What could someone **mend**?
- ○ a broken toy
- ○ a new book
- ○ a red apple

7 If you **peered** out a window, what would you be doing?
- ○ throwing
- ○ looking
- ○ leaning

cut

color

think

purple

trim

trees   violet

look   plants

light

listen   watch

focus

lavender

prune

Teacher: Read aloud the vocabulary words on each glass. Have children read the words on the pitcher and write each word under its related vocabulary word. Ask children which words they wrote on each glass and why.

Listen. Read. Write.

1 What a great **combination**! Ham, potatoes, _____ eggs make a tasty breakfast.

or
without
and

2 I like the color **lavender**. That's because I like _____ colors.

bright
light
dark

3 You need to **focus** on what I am saying. Please _____ at me when I am talking.

look
point
laugh

4 Let's **compromise**. You _____ always have things your way.

can
can't
will

5 I **improved** my story. I changed it so the ending was _____.

worse
longer
better

Teacher: Read aloud each pair of sentences. Have children read the word choices and write the best word to fill in the blank. Ask children which words they chose and why.

75

My dad loves to grow things. He works hard in his garden and never wastes time. He waters. He pulls weeds. He even trims the bushes.

Every year Dad's garden looks better. Dad plants a mix of flowers in all colors and sizes.

Once, the rabbits were eating the flowers in Dad's garden. He had to figure out what to do. He put other food out for the rabbits. Then they were happy and so was Dad.

prunes

compromise

trifles

improves

combination

1 Dad never _____ in his garden.

2 Dad _____ the bushes.

3 Every year Dad's garden _____.

4 Dad plants a _____ of flowers.

5 Dad had to _____ to solve his rabbit problem.

Teacher: Have children read the story. Then read the vocabulary words aloud. Have children read the sentences and write the vocabulary word that best completes each sentence. Ask children which words they wrote and why.

1   Which is something you could do to **improve** a fence?
- ○ rip it
- ○ cut it
- ○ paint it

2   Which tool could someone use to **prune** a tree?
- ○ a saw
- ○ a brush
- ○ a hose

3   Which might your teacher say if you were **trifling**?
- ○ You are doing a great job.
- ○ You are working too hard.
- ○ You should get back to work.

4   Which might you say if you wanted to **compromise**?
- ○ I won't do that.
- ○ Let's talk about it.
- ○ Do it my way.

5   Which is something that might be **lavender**?
- ○ a flower
- ○ an apple
- ○ a banana

6   Which is something that would be hard to **focus** on?
- ○ a boring game
- ○ an exciting book
- ○ a good movie

7   Which food would be a strange **combination**?
- ○ a coconut
- ○ a bowl of chocolate sauce
- ○ a peanut butter and spaghetti sandwich

prowl   tremble

fragile   fragrant   scorch

persistent

inventive

1

_____

2

_____

3

_____

4

_____

Teacher: Read aloud the vocabulary words. Have children look at each picture and write the vocabulary word that best describes it. Ask children which word they wrote under each picture and why.

Every day, Black Cat tried to catch the mouse that lived in the yard. Black Cat walked slowly and quietly. But every time he got close, the mouse ran under the fence. He did this again and again, but the mouse always got away.

One day, Black Cat decided to jump over the fence. Crash! He fell into all of the flowerpots and nice-smelling flowers. The pots were in pieces. The noise scared Black Cat so much that he started shaking. And the mouse got away again!

tremble

fragile

fragrant

prowled

persistent

1 Every day, Black Cat _____ through the yard.

2 Black Cat was _____.

3 The flowerpots were _____.

4 The flowers were _____.

5 The noise made Black Cat _____.

Teacher: Have children read the story. Then read the vocabulary words aloud. Have children read the sentences and write the vocabulary word that best completes each sentence. Ask children which words they wrote and why.

Listen. Write.

1 Marcos was roasting marshmallows with his mom and dad. His first marshmallow got **scorched**.

scorched

2 Marcos wasn't sure what to do next, but he decided to be **persistent**.

persistent

3 After a few tries, Marcos thought of an **inventive** way to roast the perfect marshmallow.

inventive

Teacher: Read aloud each numbered item. Have children write the vocabulary word under the picture that shows its meaning. Ask children which picture they chose and why.

1 In which place would an animal probably **prowl**?
- ○ at a party
- ○ in school
- ○ in the woods

2 What might make you **tremble**?
- ○ a loud crash of thunder
- ○ quiet rain
- ○ gentle wind blowing through the trees

3 If something is **fragile**, what should you do with it?
- ○ throw it to a friend
- ○ find out if it smells good
- ○ be very careful with it

4 What might cause something to **scorch**?
- ○ leaving it on a hot stove
- ○ leaving it outside
- ○ leaving it in hot water

5 If something is **fragrant**, what might you say?
- ○ That looks so pretty!
- ○ That smells so good!
- ○ That feels so soft!

6 If a boy is **persistent**, what does he do?
- ○ tries anything once
- ○ tries a few times
- ○ never gives up

7 If a girl is **inventive**, what does she do?
- ○ plays games she already knows
- ○ makes up new games
- ○ learns games from others

1 Julia planted flowers in her garden. She chose **crimson** flowers because she thought they would look the prettiest.

crimson

2 Sam Squirrel worked hard all day. Then he sat down to enjoy a **hearty** dinner.

hearty

3 There was a big rainstorm. The cars on the road formed a **caravan**. Then everyone could drive more safely.

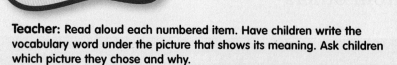

caravan

Teacher: Read aloud each numbered item. Have children write the vocabulary word under the picture that shows its meaning. Ask children which picture they chose and why.

Listen. Read. Write.

Impatient

Tradition

Nourish

1

_____ the Baby

Steve liked to help take care of his baby sister, Kayla. Steve fed Kayla lots of fruits and vegetables. Steve knew it was important for Kayla to eat healthy foods.

2

A Holiday _____

The Fourth of July was Tai's favorite holiday. Every year his family enjoyed a big picnic. But Tai's very favorite part of the holiday was at night. Tai loved the fireworks best of all!

3

TINA GETS _____ !

It was the first day of school. Tina couldn't wait to get there, but her brother was as slow as a turtle! Tina checked the clock again and again. Finally she ran to the door and yelled, "Hurry up! We have to go NOW!"

Teacher: Read aloud the vocabulary words at the top of the page. Have children read the stories and write a vocabulary word to complete each title. Ask children which words they chose to complete the titles and why.

83

Listen. Read. Write.

1 Miguel's coach **demanded** that he come to practice every day. The coach said, "You _____ be there!"

could
shouldn't
must

2 Mary stared at the woodpecker's **crimson** head. She was amazed by the bird's deep _____ color.

red
yellow
orange

3 The **caravan** of camels walked slowly across the hot, dry desert. It looked like one very _____ animal!

short
long
quiet

4 Tasha's family enjoyed a **hearty** Thanksgiving dinner. They all felt _____ after the meal.

full
hungry
sad

5 Max was getting **impatient** about leaving for the field trip. He wanted the class to leave _____.

later
tomorrow
now

Teacher: Read aloud each pair of sentences. Have children read the word choices and write the best word to fill in the blank. Ask children which words they chose and why.

1 When might someone **demand** something?
- ○ when nothing needs to be done
- ○ when something can wait until later
- ○ when something needs to happen right now

2 What color would a **crimson** birdhouse be?
- ○ bright blue
- ○ dark red
- ○ light green

3 What would a **caravan** of ants look like?
- ○ one or two ants
- ○ a few ants in different places
- ○ one long line of ants

4 What would a **hearty** laugh sound like?
- ○ like a heartbeat
- ○ big and loud
- ○ small and quiet

5 Which would describe someone who is **impatient**?
- ○ someone who can't wait
- ○ someone who is sleepy
- ○ someone who is hard at work

6 Which would be a **nourishing** snack?
- ○ a bowl of potato chips
- ○ a piece of chocolate candy
- ○ a handful of carrot sticks

7 Which would be a **tradition**?
- ○ having breakfast every day
- ○ cleaning your room once a week
- ○ having a family picnic every summer

1

A _____

Through the Trees

The twins were hiking with Dad. Andy took a quick look through the trees at the river below. He thought he saw something strange.

Glistening

Peek

Treasure

2

_____ in the River

Andy was excited. He shouted, "Dad! Amy! Let's go down to the river!" They all looked at what Andy had seen. There was a bright yellow rock at the bottom of the river. "I think it's gold!" said Amy.

3

_____ Gold

Andy reached in and grabbed the gold rock. It was wet and shiny. He couldn't wait to show Mom what he had found!

Teacher: Read aloud the vocabulary words at the top of the page. Have children read the stories and write a vocabulary word to complete each title. Ask children which words they chose to complete the titles and why.

Listen. Read. Write.

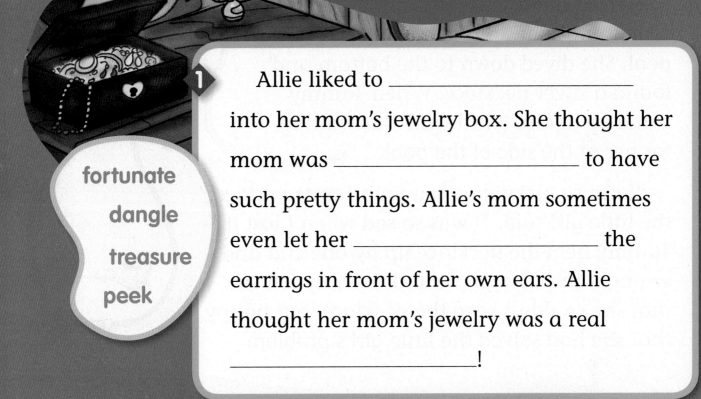

1

fortunate

dangle

treasure

peek

Allie liked to _____ into her mom's jewelry box. She thought her mom was _____ to have such pretty things. Allie's mom sometimes even let her _____ the earrings in front of her own ears. Allie thought her mom's jewelry was a real _____!

2

Jaime's stomach hurt. "You should try the _____ my mother gave me," his grandmother said. Jaime watched his grandmother pour something oily into a spoon. It _____ in the light. As Jaime swallowed, he felt the liquid _____ into his stomach. He hoped he would feel better soon.

glistened

descend

remedy

Teacher: Read aloud the vocabulary words in the shapes. Then have children read each passage and write the best words to fill in the blanks. Ask children which words they chose to complete each story and why.

When Tammy was swimming, she saw something sparkling on the bottom of the pool. She dived down to the bottom and found a silver necklace. When Tammy came up again, a little girl was waiting for her at the side of the pool.

"I am so lucky that you found my necklace," the little girl said. "I was so sad when I lost it!" Tammy held the necklace up by one end and swung it into the girl's hand. Tammy felt sad that she couldn't keep the necklace, but happy that she had solved the little girl's problem.

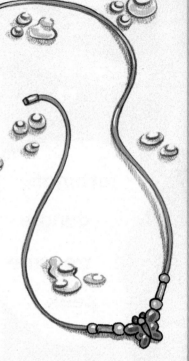

fortunate

descended

dangled

remedy

glistened

1 The necklace _____ from under the water.

2 Tammy _____ to the bottom of the pool.

3 The little girl felt _____ that Tammy found her necklace.

4 The necklace _____ from Tammy's hand.

5 Getting her necklace back was a _____ for the little girl's problem.

Teacher: Have children read the story. Then read the vocabulary words aloud. Have children read the sentences and write the vocabulary word that best completes each sentence. Ask children which words they wrote and why.

1 Which girl is **peeking**?
- ○ a girl staring out a window
- ○ a girl reading a book
- ○ a girl spying from behind a door

2 Which one might be a **treasure**?
- ○ some special coins
- ○ a blank piece of paper
- ○ some rotten eggs

3 Which one might **glisten**?
- ○ a piece of dry toast
- ○ a purple rug
- ○ a wet road

4 Which one **dangles**?
- ○ a slide
- ○ a swing
- ○ a ball

5 Which one is **descending**?
- ○ someone walking up some stairs
- ○ someone walking down some stairs
- ○ someone walking out a door

6 Which one means the same as **fortunate**?
- ○ lucky
- ○ busy
- ○ silly

7 Which boy needs a **remedy**?
- ○ a boy who scraped his knee
- ○ a boy who rode his bike
- ○ a boy who ate his lunch

1

_____ **AT LAST**

Impressed

Redeems

Heroic

When Maria's family went whale watching, for hours all they saw was blue water. Everyone was bored. Then suddenly, a huge whale leaped into the air and splashed down into the water. Maria shouted, "That was the most amazing thing I've ever seen!"

2

A _____ Rescue

It was a calm day at the beach when all of a sudden there were screams from the water. The lifeguard quickly swam out to bring a little boy back to the shore. The lifeguard saved the day!

3

Jordan _____ Himself

Jordan was running on the playground when he knocked Ryan down. Jordan felt really sorry and wished he could make things better. He played with Ryan for the rest of recess. Soon they were good friends!

Teacher: Read aloud the vocabulary words at the top of the page. Have children read the stories and write a vocabulary word to complete each title. Ask children which words they chose to complete the titles and why.

Listen. Read. Write.

precious

regret

heroic

sad

courage

mistake

brave

cuddly

cute

sorry

wrong

strong

sweet

lovable

hero

Teacher: Read aloud the vocabulary words that appear on each grocery bag. Have children read the words on the fruit and write each word under its related vocabulary word. Ask children which words they wrote on each bag and why.

Listen. Read. Write.

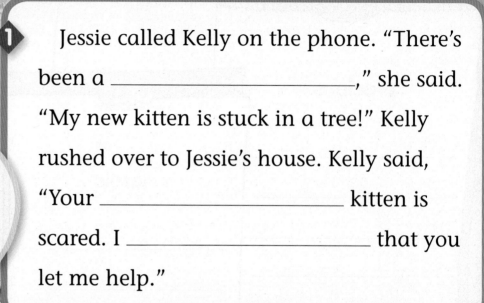

1
Jessie called Kelly on the phone. "There's been a _____," she said. "My new kitten is stuck in a tree!" Kelly rushed over to Jessie's house. Kelly said, "Your _____ kitten is scared. I _____ that you let me help."

precious

insist

calamity

2
Kelly climbed into the tree to get the kitten. Jessie thought Kelly was very _____. She was so _____ by what Kelly had done. Jessie told Kelly, "I really _____ letting my kitten climb up the tree. I hope I can _____ myself by taking better care of him from now on."

regret

redeem

impressed

heroic

92

Teacher: Read aloud the vocabulary words in the shapes. Then have children read each passage and write the best words to fill in the blanks. Ask children which words they chose to complete the story and why.

1 Which is a sentence that **insists**?
- ○ We take swimming lessons at 4:00.
- ○ Would you please feed the dog?
- ○ You need to clean your room right now!

2 Which would someone think is **precious**?
- ○ a roaring, hungry lion
- ○ a friend's new puppy
- ○ a junkyard full of cars

3 Which might someone be **impressed** by?
- ○ a piece of paper
- ○ a person climbing a ladder
- ○ a dancing elephant

4 Which might someone **regret**?
- ○ making cookies for a friend
- ○ taking a friend's favorite pencil
- ○ taking a friend to the circus

5 Which could cause a **calamity**?
- ○ playing with matches
- ○ playing with a friend
- ○ doing your homework

6 Which person is **heroic**?
- ○ a student taking a test in school
- ○ a firefighter putting out a big fire
- ○ a librarian reading a book about a hero

7 When might you want to **redeem** yourself?
- ○ after taking off your coat
- ○ after walking up the stairs
- ○ after hurting a friend's feelings

magnificent

collaborate

inquisitive

marooned   futile

plunge

protest

1

_____

2

_____

3

_____

4

_____

Teacher: Read aloud the vocabulary words. Have children look
at each picture and write the vocabulary word that best describes
it. Ask children which word they wrote under each picture and why.

Listen. Read. Write.

1   Our new puppy pokes his nose into everything. We named him Nosy. Nosy is very _____. It's _____ to try to make him stop. When we went to the lake, Nosy _____ into the cold water, but he didn't like it. Nosy _____ for a minute. Then he ran off to look at something else.

protested
inquisitive
plunged
futile

2   What if you were _____ on an island with a friend? At first it might be fun. You could enjoy the _____ sights and sounds. But how would you both get home? You and your friend could _____ to find a way.

collaborate
magnificent
marooned

Teacher: Read aloud the vocabulary words in the shapes. Then have children read each passage and write the best words to fill in the blanks. Ask children which words they chose to complete each story and why.

Frank and Fred were two little frogs who lived next to a pond. One day a toy boat floated by. Frank and Fred hopped into the boat. They floated until the boat got caught on some branches.

"Oh, no! We're stuck!" cried Fred.

"We can rock the boat until it breaks loose," said Frank.

"That will never work," said Fred.

The two frogs worked together to think of a new plan. They jumped into the water, then swam to shore. Soon they were home safely.

marooned

collaborated

protested

futile

plunged

1 When the boat got stuck, the frogs were

_____.

2 Fred thought rocking the boat would be

_____.

3 Fred _____ Frank's idea.

4 The frogs _____ to come up with

a new plan.

5 They _____ into the water and swam home.

Teacher: Have children read the story. Then read the vocabulary words aloud. Have children read the sentences and write the vocabulary word that best completes each sentence. Ask children which words they wrote and why.

96

1 If you were **marooned**, what might you do?
- ○ go to the store
- ○ think of a way to get home
- ○ ride a roller coaster

2 If you were **inquisitive**, what might you do?
- ○ ask a lot of questions
- ○ have a party in the park
- ○ play a game with your friends

3 If you were doing something **futile**, what might you say?
- ○ I'm so proud of this.
- ○ This is so funny!
- ○ This is a waste of time.

4 If you **plunged** into a lake, what would happen?
- ○ an earthquake
- ○ a big splash
- ○ a fish dinner

5 Which is something you might **protest**?
- ○ doing extra work
- ○ finding some money
- ○ hitting a home run

6 Which is something that might be **magnificent**?
- ○ a huge toy store
- ○ a peanut butter sandwich
- ○ a paper clip

7 Who is someone you might **collaborate** with?
- ○ a tiny baby
- ○ a person you don't know
- ○ your best friend

Teacher: Read aloud each numbered item and have children fill in the bubble next to the correct answer.

Words I Have Learned

A

advice
aim
ambition
announce
assorted
assume

B

bewilder
brilliant

C

calamity
caravan
chaos
cling
coax
collaborate
combat
combination
comforting
command
compassion
compete

compromise
concoction
confident
confirm
contribute
convince
cooperate
courtesy
cozy
creative
crimson
crouch
crumble

D

dangle
declare
defeat
demand
dependable
descend
details
dignified
diplomat
disaster
discover

E

edge
elegant
exaggerate
exceptional
exclaim
expression

F

faithful
famous
feast
fierce
fleet
flustered
focus
fortunate
fraction
fragile
fragrant
futile

G

gallery
generous
glee
glimmer
glisten
gracious
grateful
groom

H

handsome
hearty
hectic
heroic
honorable
host
humane
humble
humorous

I

illusion
impatient
impressed
improve
indicate
infest
innovative
inquisitive
inscription
insist
inventive

L

latched
lavender
layer
lure

M

magnificent
marooned
mend
miniature
misplace
moist
motion
motivate
murmur

N

nervous
nourish

O

obstacle
opportunity
overcome
overlook

P

pale
peek
peer
perfect
persistent
persnickety
perspective
plead
pledge
plunge
prance
precious
precise
predicament
prefer
prepared
prevail
proper
protest

prowl
prune

Q

quirky

R

radiate
rare
redeem
refreshing
regret
rehearse
remedy
repair
retrieve
ridiculous
ruin

S

satisfied
scan
scorch
sensational
shelter
shriek
sketch
sly

solution
steep
stern
succulent
suggest
swelter

T

tempting
tradition
transform
treacherous
treasure
tremble
trifle

V

versatile
vital
vivid

W

weary
wistful

My Favorite Words

You can learn new words every day. Some of them you will always want to remember. So here is a place to write your favorite words!

_____   _____
_____   _____
_____   _____
_____   _____
_____   _____
_____   _____
_____   _____
_____   _____
_____   _____
_____   _____
_____   _____
_____   _____

Teacher: Invite children to tell favorite words they have learned. Ask them to explain why these words are favorites. Then have children write the words on this list. Encourage children to add to their lists as they learn to use new words, both in and out of the classroom.